Spilled Sugar

By RL Lane

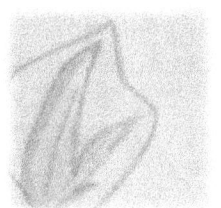

Illustrations by RL Lane

It was after midnight. I had fallen asleep. It was a strong force pulling me from my bed. I forced myself awake. I had a feeling I was going down to that basement with Tony. I didn't want to go. I wanted to sleep. I kept wondering where Axl was and why he wasn't guarding me. He seemed oblivious to it all wherever he was. There was something I did catch right at the end about sugar packets spilled on the floor. I think I slipped on them. Tony the Typesetter lived in the basement of this house at the end of his life. I will go see it tomorrow during the day. I want to see the door he showed me. The one he could push open with his hand. It had no door handle, just some kind of latch near the top that he would hold on to.

A short while later a girl appeared at the guest bedroom door. "Knock, Knock", she said. "No!" I yelled at her. I was afraid I had yelled out loud and woken Pnat's daughter across the hall. I was house sitting that weekend. I just wanted to sleep that first night. I told them I wasn't going to write about them if they were not nice to me. The voice did seem friendly in retrospect. It was a fairly young voice. I wonder who she is. I went back to sleep.

There was a woman at some point. People were looking at her as they walked by. She had her baby wrapped in a blanket. The baby was crying. She was trying to get the baby to breastfeed. She was kissing the baby on the lips to teach her how to latch on and she wasn't trying to conceal her breastfeeding. Well, I have never heard of doing that but it sort of makes sense. It is the same motion.

In the morning, the memory of the men flooded in. There was a whole group of them with burgundy short-sleeve shirts on. They were standing outside with their arms behind their backs and the hand-cuffs on. It was the scene of a drug bust. It was the daytime. There was a guy who stood out in the front. He was average height and weight, and was bald…

Welcome to Spilled Sugar. Why was it spilled? Was it an accident? Was Tony too old? Did his hands shake and drop them as he was trying to make his coffee? Or does it mean something? I am curious why they want that to be the title. Does it have something to do with the saying about spilled milk...

I looked at a lot of their family pictures while I was there. I looked hard at the happy people within the frames. I don't know what I was looking for. I just wanted to see them. Oh. I know what I was looking for. I wanted to find one that would remind me of mine. Many of them were from the wedding. I have none of my family from my unplanned Vegas wedding. Many of the pictures were getaways doing things they all loved to do. I don't think I have many of those from my married years.

My brother called me early one morning while I was there. All excited about the fish his family was catching on their camping trip in the Adirondacks of upstate NY. He went on and on about those fish and that lake. So happy to talk about the already long line of fish they had snared. He didn't once ask how I was. It made me sad until I realized how happy it made me that he would call and share the happiness...the happiness that he would have first told to our Dad if our Dad was still here. It made me so happy that I can be that for him now.

What was that saying? Something about not crying over spilled milk because you can just wipe it up and move right along. Get some more milk, or get a different kind of drink. Spilled sugar should be the same right? We can easily sweep it up. The little sparkling crystals. Sweep them up and just get some more. If it was the last packet of sugar, then get something else sweet. Some honey or a sugar substitute…

Just sweep it right up so you don't slip on it

It won't be sticky you won't even know it was there

Just keep going on

No need to even remember the accident

We all make mistakes

I am sorry I spilled it

We are after all only human

I'll try to be better

Maybe next time

When I need a packet of sugar

I'll have someone…

Who can hold my shaky hand steady. It is what I want after all…

Someone to grow old alongside…

There were no visits the second night. Where did they go, I wondered. I lie there in the bed thinking about the four of them and then I realized I had missed their messages. They are all trying to help...

Tony loved them all. He would have wanted the most for his family to be happy. That lady with her baby. Just like them. One baby girl. Protect her in her warm little blanket. Teach her to survive. The spilled sugar was an important part of the message. The sugar was already spilled. You can't change that part. You can only clean up the mess and go on. Help each other to not spill the sugar again. It should be clear. Help each other so they can go on together or just simply go on...

The happy young girl was important. Where did the happy young girl go? The laughing one in the pictures. There should be the sound of laughter bouncing off those walls. Life is not easy, my Mom said in her final letter to me, but they tried to find fun along the way. The end of her life was so hard it took me a long time to see what fun there had ever been. When I look back now, I see a lot of fun. It wasn't the fun that cost thousands of dollars. If my parents had waited for money to have fun, they would have died with frowns etched in their faces…

The last night came before I knew it. I was bombarded with messages for the future. I am not sure if they are all for me or if some are for Pnat. I have to write them in this book so I will have proof when they do come true…

A fence of stone…three layers of large stones. The stones were square shaped but not with perfect edges. The stones were so big you could walk across them. An old stone. It reminded me of Ireland. A honeymoon spot perhaps. Then there were flowers. They were odd because they didn't look like a bouquet of fresh cut flowers. They were tan and there were possibly some oranges. They weren't growing in the ground or around the stone fence. They just appeared. There is something very odd about these flowers. Then I saw a man sitting at a table with his raffle basket. He had won the RL Lane basket that contained the orange Dodge Charger car that I wrote about in EcarreT. Next, there was a thick plastic garment bag that was being unrolled. It had pieces of candy inside it instead of a suit. My soul mate had brought me back candy from his travels. Then they said "Macy". My sister has a barn cat Macy, but I don't think that is it. Then there was an old train, and a little open metal box that looked like it had metal rods in it. The men were saying something about here is where the train was powered. They had to put something inside it. Were the rods the bars of gold that Raffaele buried at his son's house? I don't think trains ran on gold back then or even now.

Then the song about raindrops that keep falling on my head. Is that just because I love the rain or to remind me of my little music box from my childhood that I carried around everywhere…it wound up to play that song…

Then finally my soul mate and I were fishing with my brother at a camp I have never seen…

I hope these all come true.

I drew four pictures on that final morning in their house…

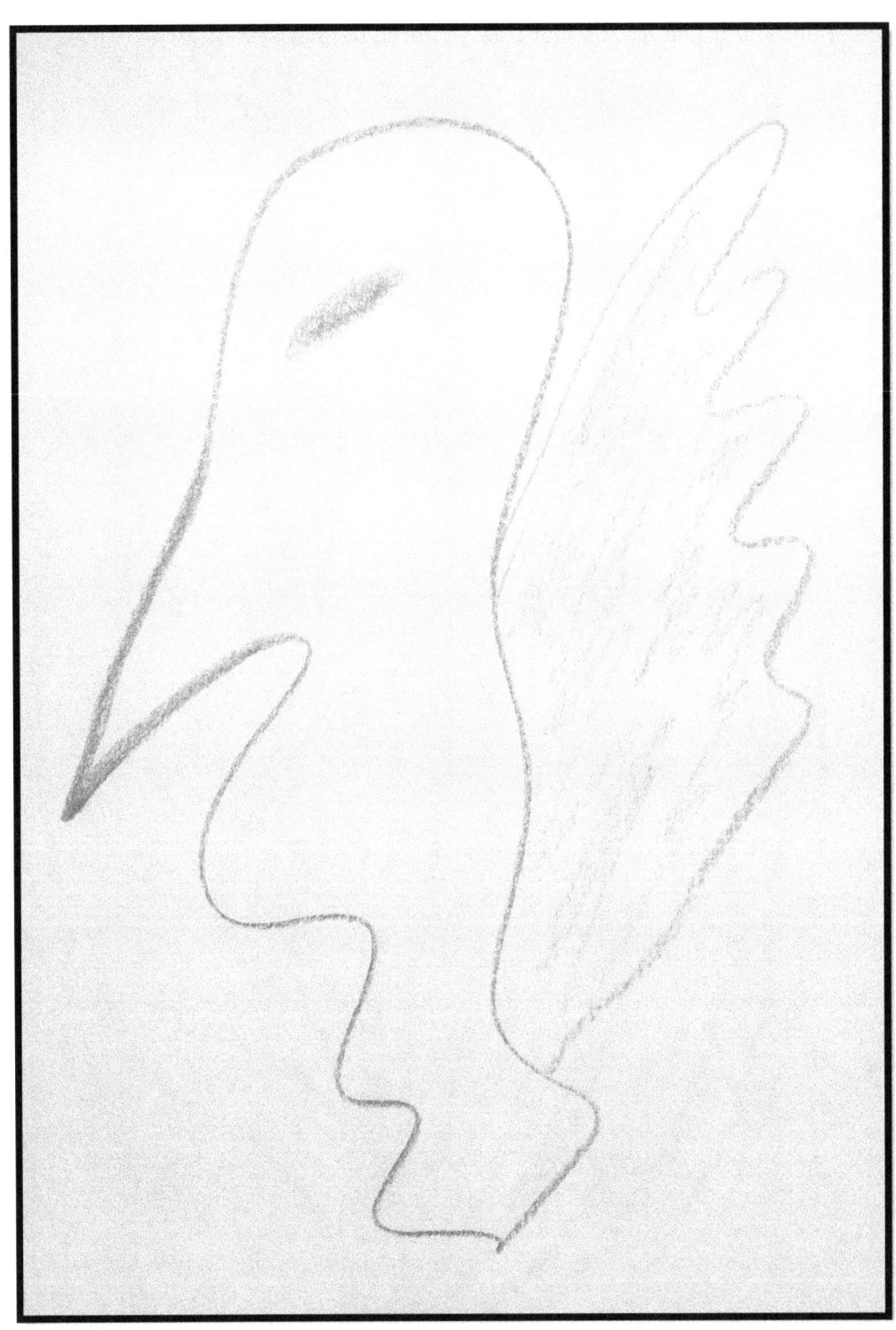

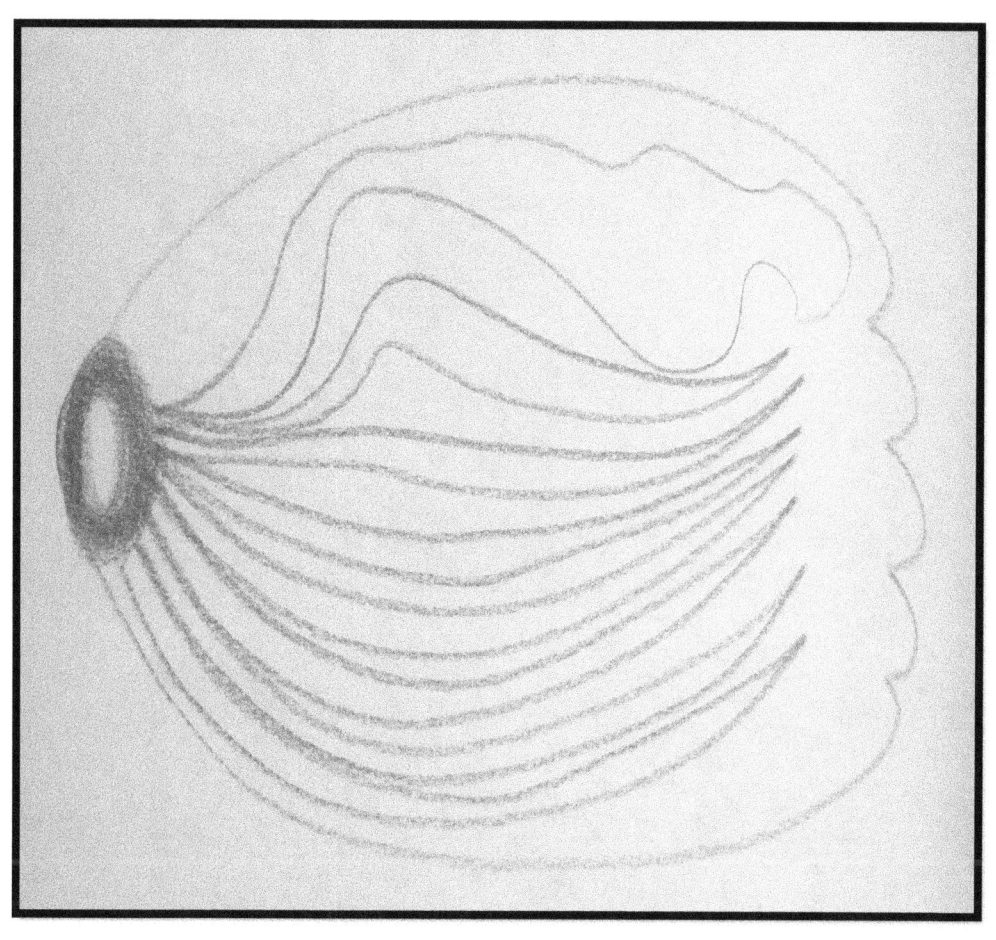

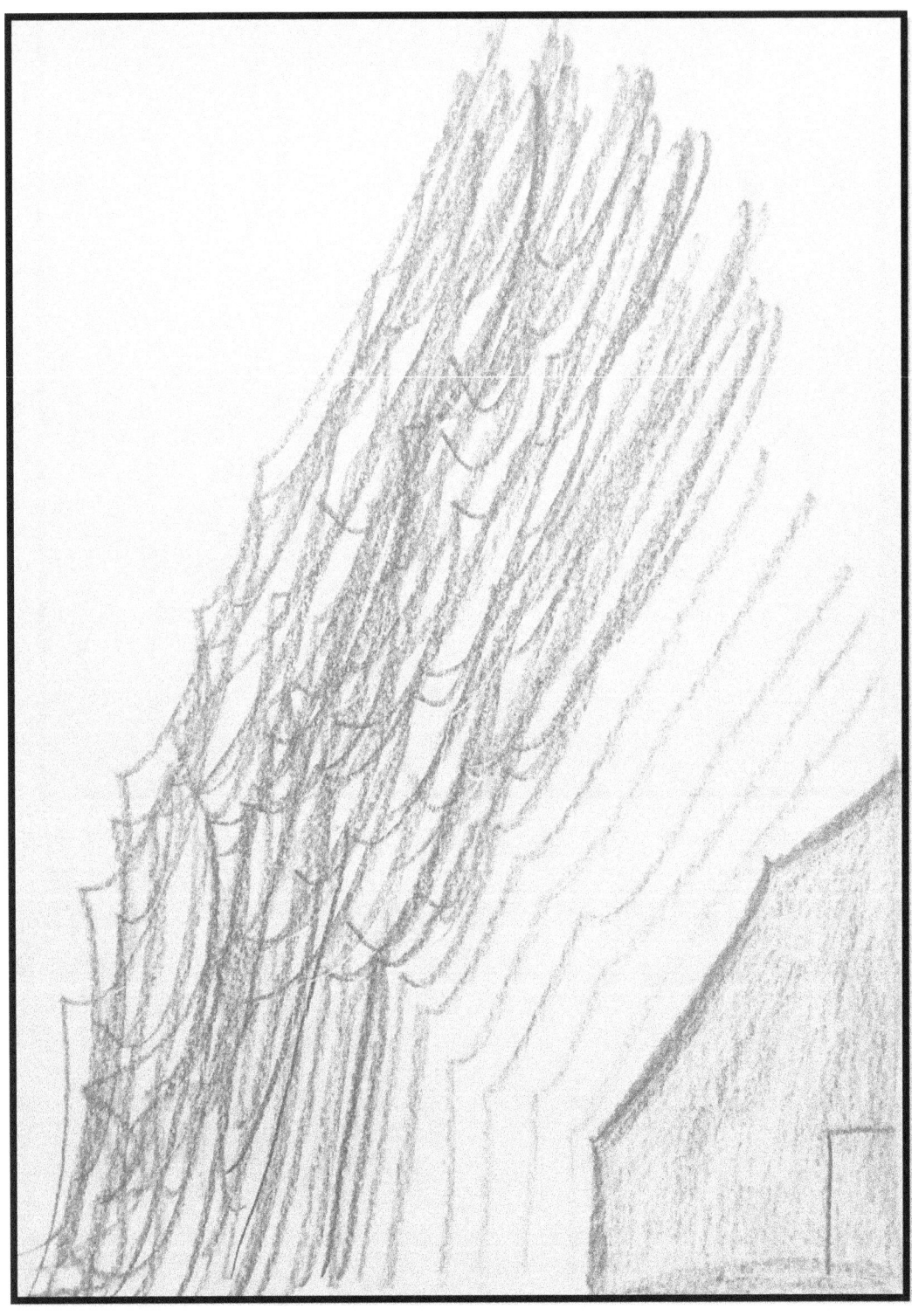

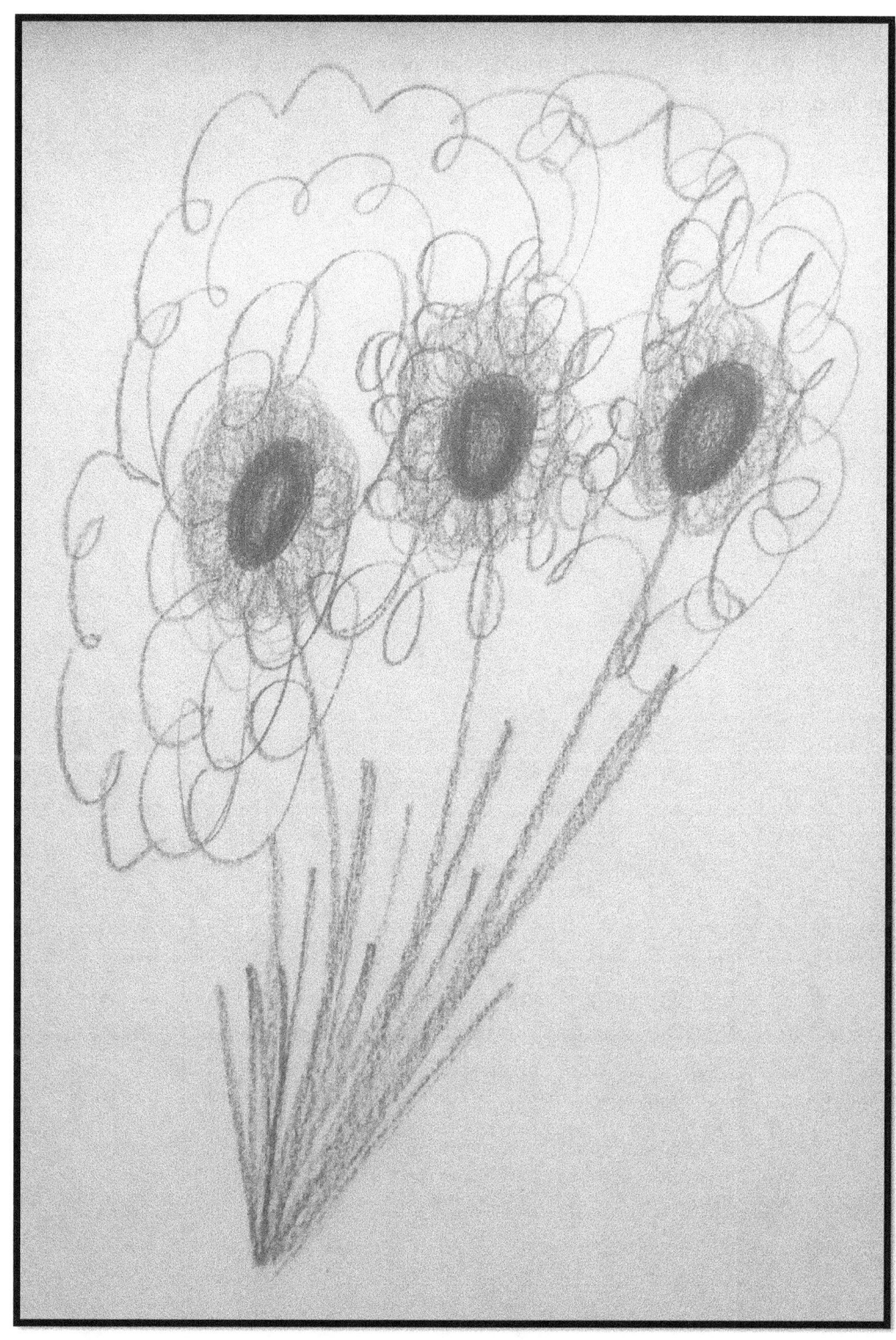

The pictures aren't really for me to interpret. They are for the people in the house. I have no doubt though that the many people watching over this house have been for a long while…

Oh. Black-Eyed Susans. That is the last picture. Black-Eyed Susans. They are important…

Oh wait. She was homeless. The lady with the baby. She had no home. How do you take care of a baby with no home? She was in a shelter as a young girl. I could feel someone else's arm lying on top of me as I slept in the crowded shelter. I pushed it away. She had to go early one morning…before the others awoke…to leave the shelter. Why? Aren't people allowed to freely leave? A shelter isn't supposed to be a permanent home…

About the Author and Illustrator

RL Lane has published the EcarreT series and a collection of short stories featuring the illustrations, along with the children's books "G" and "How to Catch a Goast". The series begins with "Chapel Street Signs"…

…unexplained connections that challenge us to beli ve. A woman, a Dad a Doctor, a cat and mouse, a horse and tale tell their stories. "Do you beli ve in spirits?" I asked my friend. "Well look", he said, "I believe there are things that cannot be explained…" Oh. Plus, hear ov a Mom's battle with her struggle to connect to the woman…her little girl.

Welcome to EcarreT…a world
Where everyone cares
Why did I have to create it in…

A fiction fantasy world?

You may already know why, but you will see regardless of what you believe as a girl's journey of love and faith on her "Touring Machine" take her on the best journey of her mundane life. A life well on its way takes a turn in a direction that could've never been seen or even dreamed…

The author can be contacted at:

RosaLeeeLane@gmail.com
www.Amazon.com/author/readrllane

Twitter.com/readrllane

Books by RL Lane

EcarreT Series:

Chapel Street Signs

secret Life OV an antE

Sri Town

Which of EcarreT

Hand of Heven

Short Stories:

Mon Treal, The Odd Cod, The Half Day, No Gift for Greed, Aunt Elm & Uncle Poc, What Would Caitlin Wear, The Bag of Scribbles, Mr. Uraly's Italy, A not G, Johnni and Georg, A Cup of Butter, The Walk of a THOUSAND Moods, Storm Window, The Rugs, Cones of Ice Crème, Angel-A, The Art of Sri Town, Under Water, The Dinner Party, The Vault, No Lines to Erase, Rock of Snow, Polka Dot Rain Boots

Children's:

G

How to Catch a Goast

www.ingramcontent.com/pod-product-compliance
Lightning Source LLC
Chambersburg PA
CBHW080629180526
45168CB00007B/3096